the EPIC GOAL WORK BOOK

EXTRAORDINARY
POWERFUL
IMPACTFUL
COURAGEOUS

Created by Anna David

LEGACY launch pad PUBLISHING

ISBN: 978-1-956955-70-5 (ebook)

ISBN: 978-1-956955-68-2 (paperback)

Scan for more information about having Anna speak at your event or organization about how EPIC failure can lead to EPIC goals.

FROM THE WORKBOOK CREATOR:

We hear a lot about S.M.A.R.T. goals—Specific, Measurable, Attainable, Relevant and Time-Sensitive. Supposedly, they can help anyone achieve anything!

Maybe they can.

But I think SMART goals are stupid. Do you want to meet just any goal? I'd much rather achieve an EPIC—Extraordinary, Powerful, Impactful and Courageous—goal. And I bet you would, too.

EPIC goals are not specific, measurable, attainable, relevant or time sensitive. They are broad, never-ending, wildly unattainable, often irrelevant and enduring.

They are things we should not be able to achieve. And yet we do.

Does achieving an EPIC goal sound too daunting? I encourage you to rewrite the story you've been telling yourself. If you're opening this workbook, perhaps you're meant to transition your thinking from "I can achieve SMART goals" to "I can achieve EPIC goals." Perhaps you're meant to discover what's possible.

Your EPIC goal doesn't need to be dramatic. It just has to be EPIC for you.

If you've been neglecting your physical and mental health, anything from quitting smoking to practicing better self-care to getting into therapy would be EPIC.

If you've been a coach potato your whole life, running a marathon would be EPIC.

If you've never been able to save, retiring on a farm could be the ultimate in EPIC.

Never been able to make more than one sale a month? Becoming the top salesperson at the company would be EPIC.

EPIC is whatever you feel is Extraordinary. Powerful, Impactful and Courageous.

Still, it has to be something you can take steps toward. "I want to win the lottery" is not an EPIC goal. "When I retire, I want to live on a farm with chicken and sheep" or "I want to sign more clients every month" is.

Here's how to use this workbook:

1) Come up with an EPIC goal. If you can't narrow it down to one, come up with more than one, although I recommend limiting it to three. (You'll see that this workbook has space for many goals; that's because this is a book you should keep using for the rest of your life.)

2) Write down WHY you want to achieve the goal. Is it so that you can finally do what you've always known in your soul you should? Is it to make more money so that you can spend more time with your family? Write your answer(s) down.

3) Describe, in present tense, your life once you've achieved your goal. How does it feel, sound and smell? Are you feeling the wind as you sail during your retirement, saltwater hitting your lips? Digging into a sizzling sirloin as you and your boss celebrate the fact that your sales have quadrupled in a year? Whatever it is, describe it so that you truly feel it.

4) Write down what you're going to do to achieve your EPIC goal. Are you going to put aside $100 every week or start taking singing lessons? Reach out to 50 potential new clients a month? Start running around the block, increasing how far you go every day until you can run a marathon? Whatever it is, make a list of at least three things you'll do.

5) Find images that show life post EPIC goal and glue them into this book. Print your own photos or images you find online; tear images from magazines. Think of this workbook as your vision board holder.

6) Do 1-5 for the other goal(s) you have (if you have them).

7) Start tackling the items on your action list.

Then commit to opening this workbook once a week to soak in both your "why" and the images you selected. You might want to start an accountability group with other people who are working toward EPIC goals; it can be one other person or a bunch of people. The point is to have regular check-ins so you can help keep one another accountable.

Now here's the key: don't look at the goal for the entire month. When you read through it, assess how much progress you've made. Have you increased sales, gotten in better shape, started setting aside for retirement? Good. Or have you not stuck to what you said you'd do? No problem. It's a perfect time to re-commit. Either way, plan to come up with new action items every month.

If your goal has evolved or changed substantially since you first came up with it, you can write it out again in the next section of this book with its new elements; doing that is only going to clarify and solidify the goal more. Find images that represent your revised goal and glue them into the pages that follow.

Now put this workbook away again but continue to regularly tackle the items on your action list. Only look at your "why" and images once a month. Soon, you'll be so connected to your "why"—and accustomed to your action list—that keeping up your EPIC goal tasks will be organic and you'll only note your progress on that goal once a year.

If you keep at this, I promise your results will turn out to be far greater than you could have ever conceived of.

Now, here's the rub: this isn't always going to be a delightful experience. Sometimes you'll see that things are not going as well as you'd like—maybe not even as well as they were a month or six months before. If that's the case, I guarantee the reason is that you're not being patient and/or you've been pushing too hard to meet your EPIC goal.

You may be asking...Isn't pushing what this is all about?

Well, yes and no. Since the universe has a much bigger plan for us than we have for ourselves, this process is about suiting up, showing up and letting go of the results. When we decide that we need things to happen a certain way—a specific relationship needs to work, a certain sale has to close, an exact marathon time has to be reached—we're missing all the "this is working" signs along the way while also strangling what the universe is trying to do for us.

Perhaps no one has summarized this concept better than spiritual leader David Hawkins when he wrote in his seminal book, *Letting Go*, "We get what we want when we stop insisting on it."

See, when we decide we need something to happen in a specific way, inherent in that is the fear that it won't happen. Think about it: "I need to make 50 sales this month" isn't too far from "What will happen if I don't?"

And here's the thing about the universe: it doesn't know the difference between a desire and a fear; in other words, put fear out there and it's as good as wishing for the things you don't want.

When you learn to set an EPIC goal, feel what it's like to achieve it, take steps forward and then let the universe take over, you'll learn how to get so much more than what you want.

It's not an overnight process. It requires ambition, patience and faith.

But the results are EPIC.

—*Anna David, your guide to EPICness*

PS I speak at events and organizations about how EPIC failure can lead to EPIC goals. If you're interested in having me speak at yours, please visit www.annadavid.com/epic.

GOAL

Date _____

_____

_____

_____

_____

_____

Write down the reason(s) why you want to achieve this goal.

_____

_____

_____

_____

_____

_____

_____

_____

_____

_____

_____

_____

_____

_____

_____

_____

_____

_____

_____

_____

Describe in present tense what it will be like to have achieved your goal.
How does your life feel, sound and smell?

What actions are you going to take to achieve your goal?

Glue images that represent your goal on this page.

Glue images that represent your goal on this page.

1 month progress

_____
_____
_____
_____
_____
_____
_____
_____
_____
_____
_____
_____
_____

What actions are you going to take over the next month to achieve your goal?

_____
_____
_____
_____
_____
_____
_____
_____
_____
_____
_____
_____

2 months progress

_____

_____

_____

_____

_____

_____

_____

_____

_____

_____

_____

_____

_____

What actions are you going to take over the next month to achieve your goal?

_____

_____

_____

_____

_____

_____

_____

_____

_____

_____

_____

_____

3 months progress

_____
_____
_____
_____
_____
_____
_____
_____
_____
_____
_____

What actions are you going to take over the next month to achieve your goal?

_____
_____
_____
_____
_____
_____
_____
_____
_____
_____
_____

4 months progress

_____

What actions are you going to take over the next month to achieve your goal?

_____

5 months progress

_____
_____
_____
_____
_____
_____
_____
_____
_____
_____
_____
_____

What actions are you going to take over the next month to achieve your goal?

_____
_____
_____
_____
_____
_____
_____
_____
_____
_____
_____

6 months progress

_____

What actions are you going to take over the next month to achieve your goal?

_____

7 months progress

_____

_____

_____

_____

_____

_____

_____

_____

_____

_____

_____

_____

What actions are you going to take over the next month to achieve your goal?

_____

_____

_____

_____

_____

_____

_____

_____

_____

_____

_____

8 months progress

_____
_____
_____
_____
_____
_____
_____
_____
_____
_____
_____
_____
_____

What actions are you going to take over the next month to achieve your goal?

_____
_____
_____
_____
_____
_____
_____
_____
_____
_____
_____
_____
_____

What actions are you going to take over the next month to achieve your goal?

What actions are you going to take over the next month to achieve your goal?

11 months progress

_____
_____
_____
_____
_____
_____
_____
_____
_____
_____
_____
_____

What actions are you going to take over the next month to achieve your goal?

_____
_____
_____
_____
_____
_____
_____
_____
_____
_____
_____
_____

1 year progress

_____
_____
_____
_____
_____
_____
_____
_____
_____
_____
_____
_____
_____

2 years progress

_____
_____
_____
_____
_____
_____
_____
_____
_____
_____
_____
_____
_____

3 years progress

4 years progress

5 years progress

6 years progress

7 years progress

8 years progress

9 years progress

10 years progress

GOAL

Date _____

_____

_____

_____

_____

_____

Write down the reason(s) why you want to achieve this goal.

_____

_____

_____

_____

_____

_____

_____

_____

_____

_____

_____

_____

_____

_____

_____

_____

_____

_____

_____

Describe in present tense what it will be like to have achieved your goal.
How does your life feel, sound and smell?

What actions are you going to take to achieve your goal?

Glue images that represent your goal on this page.

1 month progress

_____

_____

_____

_____

_____

_____

_____

_____

_____

_____

_____

What actions are you going to take over the next month to achieve your goal?

_____

_____

_____

_____

_____

_____

_____

_____

_____

_____

_____

2 months progress

_____
_____
_____
_____
_____
_____
_____
_____
_____
_____
_____
_____
_____

What actions are you going to take over the next month to achieve your goal?

_____
_____
_____
_____
_____
_____
_____
_____
_____
_____
_____
_____

3 months progress

_____
_____
_____
_____
_____
_____
_____
_____
_____
_____
_____

What actions are you going to take over the next month to achieve your goal?

_____
_____
_____
_____
_____
_____
_____
_____
_____
_____

4 months progress

What actions are you going to take over the next month to achieve your goal?

5 months progress

_____

_____

_____

_____

_____

_____

_____

_____

_____

What actions are you going to take over the next month to achieve your goal?

_____

_____

_____

_____

_____

_____

_____

_____

_____

_____

_____

_____

6 months progress

_____

What actions are you going to take over the next month to achieve your goal?

_____

7 months progress

_____
_____
_____
_____
_____
_____
_____
_____
_____
_____
_____

What actions are you going to take over the next month to achieve your goal?

_____
_____
_____
_____
_____
_____
_____
_____
_____
_____
_____

8 months progress

What actions are you going to take over the next month to achieve your goal?

9 months progress

What actions are you going to take over the next month to achieve your goal?

What actions are you going to take over the next month to achieve your goal?

_____
_____
_____
_____
_____
_____
_____
_____
_____
_____
_____

What actions are you going to take over the next month to achieve your goal?

_____
_____
_____
_____
_____
_____
_____
_____
_____
_____
_____

1 year progress

_____
_____
_____
_____
_____
_____
_____
_____
_____
_____
_____
_____

2 years progress

_____
_____
_____
_____
_____
_____
_____
_____
_____
_____
_____
_____

3 years progress

4 years progress

5 years progress

6 years progress

7 years progress

8 years progress

9 years progress

10 years progress

GOAL

Date _____

_____

_____

_____

_____

Write down the reason(s) why you want to achieve this goal.

_____

_____

_____

_____

_____

_____

_____

_____

_____

_____

_____

_____

_____

_____

_____

_____

_____

_____

_____

Describe in present tense what it will be like to have achieved your goal.
How does your life feel, sound and smell?

What actions are you going to take to achieve your goal?

Glue images that represent your goal on this page.

What actions are you going to take over the next month to achieve your goal?

_____
_____
_____
_____
_____
_____
_____
_____
_____
_____
_____
_____

What actions are you going to take over the next month to achieve your goal?

_____
_____
_____
_____
_____
_____
_____
_____
_____
_____
_____
_____
_____

3 months progress

_____

_____

_____

_____

_____

_____

_____

_____

_____

_____

_____

What actions are you going to take over the next month to achieve your goal?

_____

_____

_____

_____

_____

_____

_____

_____

_____

_____

_____

_____

_____

4 months progress

What actions are you going to take over the next month to achieve your goal?

---

5 months progress

What actions are you going to take over the next month to achieve your goal?

6 months progress

_____

_____

_____

_____

_____

_____

_____

_____

_____

_____

_____

_____

What actions are you going to take over the next month to achieve your goal?

_____

_____

_____

_____

_____

_____

_____

_____

_____

_____

_____

_____

What actions are you going to take over the next month to achieve your goal?

8 months progress

_____

_____

_____

_____

_____

_____

_____

_____

_____

_____

_____

_____

What actions are you going to take over the next month to achieve your goal?

_____

_____

_____

_____

_____

_____

_____

_____

_____

_____

_____

9 months progress

_____
_____
_____
_____
_____
_____
_____
_____
_____
_____
_____
_____

What actions are you going to take over the next month to achieve your goal?

_____
_____
_____
_____
_____
_____
_____
_____
_____
_____
_____
_____

What actions are you going to take over the next month to achieve your goal?

11 months progress

_____
_____
_____
_____
_____
_____
_____
_____
_____
_____

What actions are you going to take over the next month to achieve your goal?

_____
_____
_____
_____
_____
_____
_____
_____
_____
_____
_____
_____

1 year progress

_____

_____

_____

_____

_____

_____

_____

_____

_____

_____

_____

_____

2 years progress

_____

_____

_____

_____

_____

_____

_____

_____

_____

_____

_____

_____

3 years progress

4 years progress

5 years progress

6 years progress

7 years progress

8 years progress

9 years progress

10 years progress

GOAL

Date _____

_____

_____

_____

_____

_____

Write down the reason(s) why you want to achieve this goal.

_____

_____

_____

_____

_____

_____

_____

_____

_____

_____

_____

_____

_____

_____

_____

_____

_____

_____

_____

_____

_____

_____

Describe in present tense what it will be like to have achieved your goal.
How does your life feel, sound and smell?

What actions are you going to take to achieve your goal?

Glue images that represent your goal on this page.

1 month progress

_____
_____
_____
_____
_____
_____
_____
_____
_____
_____
_____
_____

What actions are you going to take over the next month to achieve your goal?

_____
_____
_____
_____
_____
_____
_____
_____
_____
_____
_____
_____

2 months progress

_____
_____
_____
_____
_____
_____
_____
_____
_____
_____
_____
_____

What actions are you going to take over the next month to achieve your goal?

_____
_____
_____
_____
_____
_____
_____
_____
_____
_____
_____
_____
_____
_____
_____

3 months progress

_____
_____
_____
_____
_____
_____
_____
_____
_____
_____
_____
_____
_____
_____
_____

What actions are you going to take over the next month to achieve your goal?

_____
_____
_____
_____
_____
_____
_____
_____
_____
_____
_____
_____
_____

4 months progress

_____
_____
_____
_____
_____
_____
_____
_____
_____
_____
_____
_____

What actions are you going to take over the next month to achieve your goal?

_____
_____
_____
_____
_____
_____
_____
_____
_____
_____
_____
_____
_____

5 months progress

_____

_____

_____

_____

_____

_____

_____

_____

_____

_____

_____

_____

What actions are you going to take over the next month to achieve your goal?

_____

_____

_____

_____

_____

_____

_____

_____

_____

_____

_____

6 months progress

_____
_____
_____
_____
_____
_____
_____
_____
_____
_____
_____
_____
_____

What actions are you going to take over the next month to achieve your goal?

_____
_____
_____
_____
_____
_____
_____
_____
_____
_____
_____
_____
_____

What actions are you going to take over the next month to achieve your goal?

8 months progress

What actions are you going to take over the next month to achieve your goal?

9 months progress

_____

_____

_____

_____

_____

_____

_____

_____

_____

_____

_____

What actions are you going to take over the next month to achieve your goal?

_____

_____

_____

_____

_____

_____

_____

_____

_____

_____

_____

_____

_____

_____

_____

_____

_____

_____

_____

_____

_____

_____

What actions are you going to take over the next month to achieve your goal?

_____

_____

_____

_____

_____

_____

_____

_____

_____

_____

_____

11 months progress

What actions are you going to take over the next month to achieve your goal?

1 year progress

_____

_____

_____

_____

_____

_____

_____

_____

_____

_____

_____

_____

_____

2 years progress

_____

_____

_____

_____

_____

_____

_____

_____

_____

_____

_____

_____

_____

3 years progress

4 years progress

5 years progress

6 years progress

7 years progress

8 years progress

9 years progress

10 years progress

GOAL

Date _____

_____

_____

_____

_____

Write down the reason(s) why you want to achieve this goal.

_____

_____

_____

_____

_____

_____

_____

_____

_____

_____

_____

_____

_____

_____

_____

_____

_____

_____

_____

_____

_____

Describe in present tense what it will be like to have achieved your goal.
How does your life feel, sound and smell?

What actions are you going to take to achieve your goal?

_____
_____
_____
_____
_____
_____
_____
_____
_____
_____
_____
_____
_____
_____
_____
_____
_____
_____
_____
_____
_____
_____
_____

Glue images that represent your goal on this page.

1 month progress

_____
_____
_____
_____
_____
_____
_____
_____
_____
_____
_____
_____

What actions are you going to take over the next month to achieve your goal?

_____
_____
_____
_____
_____
_____
_____
_____
_____
_____
_____
_____

2 months progress

_____

What actions are you going to take over the next month to achieve your goal?

_____

3 months progress

_____
_____
_____
_____
_____
_____
_____
_____
_____
_____
_____
_____

What actions are you going to take over the next month to achieve your goal?

_____
_____
_____
_____
_____
_____
_____
_____
_____
_____
_____
_____
_____

4 months progress

_____
_____
_____
_____
_____
_____
_____
_____
_____
_____
_____
_____
_____
_____

What actions are you going to take over the next month to achieve your goal?

_____
_____
_____
_____
_____
_____
_____
_____
_____
_____
_____
_____
_____

5 months progress

What actions are you going to take over the next month to achieve your goal?

6 months progress

_____

_____

_____

_____

_____

_____

_____

_____

_____

_____

_____

_____

_____

What actions are you going to take over the next month to achieve your goal?

_____

_____

_____

_____

_____

_____

_____

_____

_____

_____

_____

_____

_____

7 months progress

_____

_____

_____

_____

_____

_____

_____

_____

_____

_____

What actions are you going to take over the next month to achieve your goal?

_____

_____

_____

_____

_____

_____

_____

_____

_____

_____

_____

_____

_____

_____

_____

_____

_____

_____

_____

_____

_____

_____

_____

_____

What actions are you going to take over the next month to achieve your goal?

_____

_____

_____

_____

_____

_____

_____

_____

_____

_____

_____

_____

9 months progress

_____

_____

_____

_____

_____

_____

_____

_____

_____

_____

_____

_____

_____

What actions are you going to take over the next month to achieve your goal?

_____

_____

_____

_____

_____

_____

_____

_____

_____

_____

_____

_____

_____

_____

_____
_____
_____
_____
_____
_____
_____
_____
_____
_____
_____
_____
_____
_____

What actions are you going to take over the next month to achieve your goal?

_____
_____
_____
_____
_____
_____
_____
_____
_____
_____
_____
_____

11 months progress

_____
_____
_____
_____
_____
_____
_____
_____
_____
_____
_____
_____

What actions are you going to take over the next month to achieve your goal?

_____
_____
_____
_____
_____
_____
_____
_____
_____
_____
_____
_____

1 year progress

_____
_____
_____
_____
_____
_____
_____
_____
_____
_____
_____
_____
_____

2 years progress

_____
_____
_____
_____
_____
_____
_____
_____
_____
_____
_____
_____
_____
_____

3 years progress

_____

_____

_____

_____

_____

_____

_____

_____

_____

_____

_____

4 years progress

_____

_____

_____

_____

_____

_____

_____

_____

_____

_____

_____

5 years progress

6 years progress

7 years progress

8 years progress

9 years progress

10 years progress

GOAL

Date _____

_____

_____

_____

_____

_____

Write down the reason(s) why you want to achieve this goal.

_____

_____

_____

_____

_____

_____

_____

_____

_____

_____

_____

_____

_____

_____

_____

_____

_____

_____

_____

_____

_____

_____

_____

_____

Describe in present tense what it will be like to have achieved your goal.
How does your life feel, sound and smell?

What actions are you going to take to achieve your goal?

Glue images that represent your goal on this page.

1 month progress

_____
_____
_____
_____
_____
_____
_____
_____
_____
_____

What actions are you going to take over the next month to achieve your goal?

_____
_____
_____
_____
_____
_____
_____
_____
_____
_____
_____
_____

2 months progress

_____

What actions are you going to take over the next month to achieve your goal?

_____

3 months progress

_____
_____
_____
_____
_____
_____
_____
_____
_____
_____
_____
_____

What actions are you going to take over the next month to achieve your goal?

_____
_____
_____
_____
_____
_____
_____
_____
_____
_____
_____
_____

4 months progress

_____

_____

_____

_____

_____

_____

_____

_____

_____

_____

_____

_____

What actions are you going to take over the next month to achieve your goal?

_____

_____

_____

_____

_____

_____

_____

_____

_____

_____

_____

5 months progress

_____
_____
_____
_____
_____
_____
_____
_____
_____
_____
_____
_____
_____

What actions are you going to take over the next month to achieve your goal?

_____
_____
_____
_____
_____
_____
_____
_____
_____
_____
_____
_____

_____
_____
_____
_____
_____
_____
_____
_____
_____
_____
_____
_____
_____

What actions are you going to take over the next month to achieve your goal?

_____
_____
_____
_____
_____
_____
_____
_____
_____
_____
_____
_____
_____
_____

7 months progress

What actions are you going to take over the next month to achieve your goal?

What actions are you going to take over the next month to achieve your goal?

9 months progress

_____
_____
_____
_____
_____
_____
_____
_____
_____
_____
_____

What actions are you going to take over the next month to achieve your goal?

_____
_____
_____
_____
_____
_____
_____
_____
_____
_____
_____
_____

_____

_____

_____

_____

_____

_____

_____

_____

_____

_____

_____

_____

What actions are you going to take over the next month to achieve your goal?

_____

_____

_____

_____

_____

_____

_____

_____

_____

_____

_____

11 months progress

_____

_____

_____

_____

_____

_____

_____

_____

_____

_____

_____

_____

_____

What actions are you going to take over the next month to achieve your goal?

_____

_____

_____

_____

_____

_____

_____

_____

_____

_____

_____

_____

1 year progress

_____
_____
_____
_____
_____
_____
_____
_____
_____
_____
_____
_____
_____

2 years progress

_____
_____
_____
_____
_____
_____
_____
_____
_____
_____
_____
_____
_____

3 years progress

_____

_____

_____

_____

_____

_____

_____

_____

_____

_____

_____

_____

4 years progress

_____

_____

_____

_____

_____

_____

_____

_____

_____

_____

_____

_____

5 years progress

6 years progress

7 years progress

8 years progress

9 years progress

10 years progress

GOAL

Date _____

_____

_____

_____

_____

_____

Write down the reason(s) why you want to achieve this goal.

_____

_____

_____

_____

_____

_____

_____

_____

_____

_____

_____

_____

_____

_____

_____

_____

_____

_____

_____

Describe in present tense what it will be like to have achieved your goal.
How does your life feel, sound and smell?

What actions are you going to take to achieve your goal?

Glue images that represent your goal on this page.

1 month progress

_____

_____

_____

_____

_____

_____

_____

_____

_____

_____

What actions are you going to take over the next month to achieve your goal?

_____

_____

_____

_____

_____

_____

_____

_____

_____

2 months progress

_____
_____
_____
_____
_____
_____
_____
_____
_____
_____
_____
_____
_____
_____

What actions are you going to take over the next month to achieve your goal?

_____
_____
_____
_____
_____
_____
_____
_____
_____
_____
_____
_____
_____

3 months progress

_____

_____

_____

_____

_____

_____

_____

_____

_____

_____

_____

_____

What actions are you going to take over the next month to achieve your goal?

_____

_____

_____

_____

_____

_____

_____

_____

_____

_____

_____

What actions are you going to take over the next month to achieve your goal?

5 months progress

_____

_____

_____

_____

_____

_____

_____

_____

_____

_____

_____

_____

What actions are you going to take over the next month to achieve your goal?

_____

_____

_____

_____

_____

_____

_____

_____

_____

_____

_____

_____

6 months progress

_____
_____
_____
_____
_____
_____
_____
_____
_____
_____
_____
_____
_____

What actions are you going to take over the next month to achieve your goal?

_____
_____
_____
_____
_____
_____
_____
_____
_____
_____
_____
_____

What actions are you going to take over the next month to achieve your goal?

8 months progress

_____
_____
_____
_____
_____
_____
_____
_____
_____
_____
_____
_____

What actions are you going to take over the next month to achieve your goal?

_____
_____
_____
_____
_____
_____
_____
_____
_____
_____
_____
_____
_____

What actions are you going to take over the next month to achieve your goal?

What actions are you going to take over the next month to achieve your goal?

What actions are you going to take over the next month to achieve your goal?

1 year progress

2 years progress

3 years progress

4 years progress

5 years progress

6 years progress

7 years progress

8 years progress

9 years progress

10 years progress

Anna David is the *New York Times* bestselling author of eight books. She's spoken at colleges and corporations around the country, been featured at three different TEDx events and shared the stage with such global leaders as Tony Robbins. She has appeared repeatedly on *Today, The Talk, Good Morning America* and numerous other programs, where she's discussed human behavior, goals, mental health, happiness and failure. Her company, Legacy Launch Pad, writes and publishes books for entrepreneurs. She lives in Los Angeles with her boyfriend, filmmaker Jim Agnew, and their son, Benjamin.

Anna David is the *New York Times* bestselling author of eight books. She's spoken at colleges and corporations around the country, been featured at three different TEDx events and shared the stage with such global leaders as Tony Robbins. She has appeared repeatedly on *Today*, *The Talk*, *Good Morning America* and numerous other programs, where she's discussed human behavior, goals, mental health, happiness and failure. Her company, Legacy Launch Pad, writes and publishes books for entrepreneurs. She lives in Los Angeles with her boyfriend, filmmaker Jim Agnew, and their son, Benjamin.